# Dear Corporation,

# Dear Corporation,

Adam Fell

FORKLIFT_BOOKS

SECOND EDITION, MARCH 2019

Copyright © 2013 by Adam Fell

ISBN 978-0-9995931-7-2

Book and cover design by Eric Appleby

FORKLIFT_BOOKS

*Cincinnati, Ohio*

WWW.FORKLIFTBOOKS.COM

Work and learn in evil days, in insulted days, in days of debt and depression and calamity. Fight best in the shade of the cloud of arrows.

-Ralph Waldo Emerson
*Journals*

Nolite te bastardes carborundorum.

—Margaret Atwood
*The Handmaid's Tale*

# Dear
# Corporation,

## Dear
## Corporation,

Dream at night always of your loved ones in danger. Wake tangled in the gauze of your sheets. Draw yourself a hot bath. Unhood the windows. It's becoming harder and harder to tell whether the motion detector has been triggered or it's already morning. Try to practice your breathing. Let the day open up to you with the hiss of automated doors. Find something in the near distance to look forward to. Hold on. Even if the boot is crushing your fingers. Hold on. It's not the full-forced crush of anxiety that makes your legs do that aching thing, that tenderizer thing, that feral, fidgeting thing. It's the protocol, the tools of the trade, the glare of the moneybright capitol. Fuck protocol. Fuck the tools of the trade. Fuck the lone animal bullshit, the survival of the fittest. Fuck the lions in the millions, the billions, the abasement and ache of the blindly entitled. Distrust the unconflicted, the unaccountable, the unworried, the unwounded. Distrust your own impulse to leave your love in the ruins. Your pain is not the only pain, not the worst pain. Your guilt is not the only guilt, not the worst guilt. If the cop says the thirty-year-old musician he shot dead on your block was drunk, was belligerent, was reaching for the gun, be immortally suspicious. Pay closest attention to who shifts the wind. Always wonder what exactly is burning so close on the air. Smoke, now ghost-smoke, now gone. Listen everywhere, to every one, always. Make reckless, bloodbright basement music. Make blackout bedroom make-out noise. Make language like nosebleeds and rug burns and snakebites and shiners. Language like warm hands on warm chests, between warm legs. Fail ardently. Fail gloriously. Fail over and over and over again.

## Dear Corporation,

There is a calm in me here and now, an untrampling of my chest that often leads me to skin the rabbit with my love, but right now I can't help but stand still just this once sans internet connectivity and smile at how happy pink the flossblood from my mouth is when frothed with toothpaste and spit in the sink. I can't help but search for the pressurized domes and hallways of an underwater city called Rapture in the drain-dancing bubbles.

Two nights ago, my love and I stole a ladder, skittered over, and skinned the power and light from the neighboring apartment's motion detector. It had been tazing us awake through our blinds for months, and we shuttered its power in minutes. We snuck home ecstatic and groping with the adrenaline of our new, proactive possibilities. But in the morning, I was back to my burnt coffee and suet-seed toast, back to fumbling through the hours, the smoke breaks. I think I read something. I think I typed something on a screen with my fingers. Then stumbled home, dispirited and disempowered, only to find a hatchet and hammer cuddled in the kitchen, my love standing above with the most righteous tornado touching down in her eyes.

We waited until dark, stole downtown and broke into the offices of a subprime mortgage lender. We swept through the lobby, past the water feature, the woodgrain. We pressed our thumbs to the windpipes of the photographs on each lender's desk. We lost our clothes in the boardroom, swiveled in the swivel chairs, made love in many different yet equally exciting positions on the mahogany conference table, swept the conference call speakers to the floor like a lust-crashed Scrabble board from a bed. We glistened like indoor pools in the post-sex dawn. We watched the capitol wake through the skyrise windows, and asked ourselves: if we murder this place tonight, do we murder its people too? When we press our thumbs to the throats of photographic children, do we press our thumbs to the throats of their image-sakes? We asked ourselves: if we murder you tonight, my dear Corporation, will your mother weep in front of the cameras? Will your sad little brother swing alone in the cold of the playground?

## Dear
## Corporation,

I don't know how to
say how I feel poetically, or politely,
or without the jugular and collapse
of the immediate heart so, tonight,
I won't say anything at all. Just stare
out the window at our stunned little
writhe. Hold back the strongest urge
to knock out the capitol's most critical
walls, replace its fiber optic cables with
lightning bugs, replace the investment
bankers all with bunker busters. I lock
eyes with the capitol's bright and empty
rooms and admit that sometimes, deep
in my affluent, American cells, I miss
my body carved to projectile, I miss
trebuchet shoulders and knuckles flaked
to arrowheads, miss my hands massive
and molded from molten to the bolts
of ballistas. I miss blackjack and cudgel
and quarterstaff and flintlock. I miss
pummel and powder keg and pike and

I am not proud of this. I know it's not a healthy feeling. I try to disarm, to uncock. I try to practice my breathing. I try *The Master Cleanse, The Stationary Bike, The Bikram Sweat, The Contortion Stretch, The Screaming Vegan Meatloaf, The Nightly Scorching Bathtime, The Leafy Greens and Venom Television, The Self-Mutilation of a Wisconsin Winter's Run,* but we can only cleanse our bodies so much before we realize it's not our bodies that need detoxing.

## Dear
## Corporation,

It's 4:17 am and I
can't help imagining the room where
my brother is saving the computers of
Sacramento hospitals. He is thizzing
from his first corporate exhaustion,
the softbroke gnaw of nurses failing
to remember some keystroke. His
linoleum-rapped knuckles are bleeding.
He is tieless, face less furnished in the
monitor glass than his bedbug-fogged
apartment. I imagine the nurses station
as some sudden floodlit city, closed-
circuiting and compiling the gauzed,
the sutured, the limping, the aching,
the flimsy, the thank-god-thank-god-at-
deep-pharmaceutical-rest.

He can do nothing for
them but make their agonies paperless.
Third shift after third shift, he feels
that fact compacting the soft-pressed

grains of his heart like ocean-ground plastics smothering slow generations of beach. It is some godforsaken hour. It is some godforsaken chair with its arms too high. There are magazines on the end tables about making babies, taking care of babies, famous people who shouldn't be doing either. He is detox-white and waiting, scraping his hotel bar hangover off on the mute architecture, ghost-riding the whip of some disused wheelchair toward the nearest flight to leave. *Chopped and screwed,* he whispers through the fan blades, *I am chopped and screwed.* And then he's lobbed from the cab at dawn, reaching out for the hotel, through the hiss of automated doors, only to find endless hallways of suites where robber barons sleep bloated with their mistresses, their rooms clotted with coarse-pilled shit, shredded newspaper, some sort of massive hamster bottle in the corner for sucking. It is because he is softer that he will succeed, because he is kinder that his rouseless snorings will siren through every hotel wall, will startle every robber baron to wake defused of their hard-ons, their deficit eyes glared as senseless as touchscreens, their golden parachutes torn shallow to shreds. They will scream, they will cry, they will threaten litigation, they will bang the shit out of his thick walls and snitch to the concierge, but his kindness will sleep him soundly, will wake him always a moment before the wake-up call, will tender him just tender enough to redefine the achings inside.

My dear Corporation, it's 4:39 am, and here in Wisconsin, I am falling asleep on the couch. I imagine Tyler as finally safe for the moment, newday-hatched in a lawn of hotel linen. A small, bellied child again, lying next to me on the beach blanket, sleeping soundly through the fireworks.

# Dear Corporation,

I've been meaning to compose a thoughtful, intelligent message to see how you've been and impress you into wanting to write to me again but my apartment is on fire and the fan isn't helping and the rain only quells where its drops hit directly. It's been over a year since I met you on the mountain, a year since I lit your cigarette in the felsenmeer and the fog-eyed tourists in the cog railway car goggled at us like *we* were the toothless tigers pacing behind green electricities. That was the first time we spoke. And the last. I apologize for that, but it's mostly your fault. If we could just bend the subway tracks this way, we could slog the summer city, mush our sled dogs through the plow heaps of humidity, and unmuzzle ourselves at the Crystal Corner. I prefer bourbon and soda, and, just so you know, yes, eventually the blood will stop pouring. Sometimes the health falls back to us when we don't want anything to do with it, which can be good: the blood, the beatings, the close-in gut and shiv of the immediate heart. But we can never really understand the Nazca lines of soft damage inside us until we're far enough above, until we've learned that we can never really leave each other, no matter how hard we try, no matter how many bodies we lay in between.

# Dear
# Corporation,

Tyger, listen, we're burning too bright already, what more do you want, you sadist? We are sad, lonely, often skillfully so. We obsess about particular people, trawl our tangled idea of them through our brains or drive them into our brains with nail guns. It's just these people, the people we love, *our* people, they sink deep and seep in and it's as if we're drowning in that moment, when our throats open fully and cannot close, the moment when the imminent becomes the invincible, and we are awash again in the era of red electricities that lived in our lungs before lightning. We brood and we bray and we simmer. We collapse whole days plying ourselves open like expressways buckled with ice. We just want someone we want to make breakfast for, is that too much to ask? But the people we could love lately are fucking others, and those others are mostly fuckers, and the people we are fucking we never wanted to make breakfast for in the first place. Tyger, there are no curatives for what we got. There is no dousing bell for these catacomb flames. No pestled and powdered snow leopard bones, or elephant tusks, no possible restorative use for those poor dead rhinos and their grizzly hacked-off horns. *That* is what our burning looks like, Tyger, fresh from the slaughter, straight to the market, chased through the jungle by engines of our own design. We are all possessor and possessed. We all have millennia of dirty oceans sleeking the unraveled baleen of our hair. There is always blood on our tiles, in our tubs, on the hardwood, the cracked linoleum, always blood doused from our broken noses, our split lips, misted from our lungs, seeping from our self-inflicted wounds into the snow, into the drying grass, onto the parking lots and pavements of our capitol city, blackout city, Invisible City, Inoculated City, Erotic City, Dark City, Fist City, Rivet City, Devil in the White City, Suffragette City, Stories from the City, Shining Violence in the City, The City & The City, Language City, Goron City, Ybor City, Ideal City, Atlantic City, Angela Surf City, Clash City, Crescent City, Sin City, City 17, City of White Donkeys, City of Lost Children, City of God, City in Progress, City of Dreams, Tiny City Made of Ashes, City Full of Sissy, Pretty Love, Sissy, Pretty Love, Sissy, Pretty Love, yeah, all swerving and streaked in the sordid dark of our staggers. Tyger, please, just stop. I don't care what you are trying to say, I just can't fight this feeling anymore, just say the word, please just say the motherfucking word and I swear to god I'll burn every bloodbright city of Santorums to the ground and make Pagels and Dillons and Demskes of it all. I have killed for love and I will kill again.

# Dear Corporation,

My love, before you, this dehydrated piss of mine was such a lonely shade-grown coffee, my semen's judgment clouded with eerie, evangelical determination. My eyes were broken touchscreens, I tasted my own blood in every daiquiri. But now, no matter where I am, I can hear the creaking of the pier beneath your spectacular breasts, I can feel the sway of your waves cupping my sack of indestructible puppies. Collisions like ours are a shock to every system. Politicians never counted on us. Wall Street never counted on us. The cadaverous yuppies and their screaming vegan babies never counted on us. Investment bankers swear they keep finding our faces burned into their zeroes and ones like belligerent, binary Marys. They feel our fingers down the throats of their housing bubbles, our teeth foreclosing on the napes of their tender, uninsured necks. To put it more delicately: I want you to fuck the fiscal responsibility out of me. I want you to fuck me until universal healthcare. We are the only thing that is too big to fail, so put down the briefcase and come skin the rabbit with me. We make such a flaring of magnificently epic nostrils, such a pure, pornographic latte. If you keep coming home, I'll keep pouring this miraculous rye that keeps the city from paving us over, that keeps us under-worn and porch-warm amongst armies of snow. Darling, you cave me like a raindrop in ash. Touch the tip of your electronic cigarette to me so I can ignite.

Dear Corporation,

the assholes say, No matter what mine is not a conspiracy of fifty-four bones, but a finally commuted sentence, an assault rifle forever jammed, crossbow bolts through each other's asses instead of the apples on our heads, then decades of ▬ lavish recuperation by the sea.

xoxo -A.

## *Dear Corporation,*

In painting after painting of Adam and Eve with the apple unbit, you recognize your own eyes of animal midnight. Intimately. You recognize the straw dog of the snake strung up in the night of their trees like some nefarious cigar. You recognize that in the highest boughs of our trees is a temptation of treason, a blackout city without reason, capable—if uncoiled—of the brightest evasions, the brightest collusions, the brightest fruit of effusions to reach up for again and again. But there is a deficit of language in their immaculate mouths, a vast unemployment in their immaculate feet. Their knees have never known the cold of the bathroom floor in midwestern December, never been up nights with each other, stomach sick, head sick, heart sick, butt sick, never had to quilt over and broth-feed and placidly bathe the shivering isles of fidelity, loyalty, anxiety, never had to douse the doubt that is the congenital defect of our sorrowing mansions, never woke in the morning to find their cloudless suncult of a friend had died in her sleep, never had to find a blanket, a box, the right strength of hands to sift through the irredeemable cold of what's left of her for what's never coming back. Adam and Eve with the apple unbit never had to admit to themselves that, while all the renaissance paintings they are in are quite beautiful, there is a squalling arctic whiteness to them that is unsettling, a privilege in the plumpness of their white angel babies that is unsettling. So many fat, white babies clouding the sky. Gull-winged babies and goldfinch babies, babies stalling the stormclouds with calm-white, dove-like wings. They are the announcers, the messengers, the stayers-of-hands. Adam and Eve with the apple unbit never had to un-coin their eyes to imbalance, inequity, the ingenuity and ignorance and incessant allure of the world. To wake in the dark of the woods and realize we have been created at all is to realize we have not always been, that we will not always be. We are not born to stake a claim, but to claim a stake in each other, to burn alive if needed in the pure resurrection of our simultaneous decay. We tell ourselves *they* had a choice, that *we* have a choice, but some choices are rolling blackouts, some choices are two frayed ends of wire arcing reddest electricities between raw, uncoiling fingers, some choices are piling sandbags with your neighbors as the floodwaters rise, some choices are not really choices at all.

# Dear Corporation,

No one likes their first cigarette. Any chaperone could tell you that. Any chaperone could tell you our peephole hearts all look out into the same midnight motel hallway where two post-prom kids forever fumble with each other's zippers. Any chaperone could tell you what happens after that is always up to you. Maybe the boy forever comes he-thinks-too-soon upon his shy date's hand. Maybe they smile at this, blush and bite and bare themselves further, their tenderness slipping under our doors like unsealed envelopes, their laughter warming the walls of our rooms. Or maybe instead of forever laughter, forever lenience, there is forever belligerence, forever shattering. Maybe the boy stalks away ashamed to dent his knuckles bloody on the khaki bathroom stall. Maybe: a boy's first stab at DMZ, a boy's first stab at quarantine. What if his mother taught him this? What if his father? What if he never speaks to his shy date again? What if he has been shattered by his family into shattering himself, into shrapneling out at the world unannounced? Or, maybe, instead of shattering, instead of shame, the kids forever and always incandesce into song: *I can feel it coming in the air tonight, oh lord. I've been waiting for this moment all my life.*

## Dear Corporation,

It is the glacial span of the disordinary places we are born into that grind us to crawl inside the covers of each other and create ever-new concoctions with bourbon. My dear Corporation, are you corporeal enough tonight to reach out your hand? To spare a cigarette, a sip from your flask? How many hours of darkness are you made of? How many hours of light? It's ok. You don't have to answer us yet. But don't be ashamed of yourself either. We all blink awake at the center of the same frozen lake and must go forward. Take your time. Unbalance. Re-. You're only human. Let the words that you find give you form. Feel your deepest cables thrive with the weight of each step. Head toward the shore, the distance of lights. We'll be waiting for you by the fire.

# *Dear Corporation,*

Living in the sirens, all you want is a nightcap in a quiet dive, is that too much to ask? You miss silence. You miss sadness. You miss the knife you made a foundation. Living in the sirens, you know how lonely it is playing the perkiest tit in the mouth of panic. You want to pulp the soggy coaster beneath your Manhattan, watch the intimate rotations of patrons in the bar-back mirror, and go home alone, bourbon glown, listen to *Liquid Swords* and maybe do the dishes. But the girls down the bar keep mistaking internships for internment, keep taking Goldschläger shots and photos of themselves with the same porn-smudged, half-torn wink and smile. Living in the sirens, you know where this is going: Suck-for-a-Buck, Dum-Dum bouquets, a bile-hot headache and a marriage in the rain. You know you're right, but it's the kind of right that's a corkscrew in your throat. You imagine them stringing themselves up along the rooftops of this scalding summer city, christmas-lit and momentously martini'd, no matter whose clothes are burning beneath them on the avenue, whether anyone's pulled alive from the rubble or not.

But even after they stagger out into the migration of mass transit, after the reinforced door has muzzled the city again and no one left inside would dare crush such priceless seconds of seclusion with uncrumpled dollars of music, even then, in the voluptuous bloodbeat of the closest you have come to silence in this city, the closed-captioning on the muted television above the bartender's head reads [Sirens].

## *Dear Corporation,*

When I go for a run, the strangest violence glows out from my pores, the deep flowing ochre of morning multi-vitamin piss. I want the healthier people I pass, the thick-legged couple baby-talking their labradoodle, the lithe and shirtless runners gliding in their foot gloves, the spandex-padded cyclists and swing-pushing baby-petters, to all die horrifically for no real reason except I know I will never pass them again and that is what it means to get older: to lose more and more and within that loss try to gather a gaining. So I walk myself home in the dirty summer dawn, unhood the windows, watch the youngest construction workers stretch like waking wolves in the soft, smoking tar. I mix myself a nice stiff Sazerac from the recipe I clipped from Nate:

*2 oz rye whiskey*
*¼ oz. sugar syrup (2:1 sugar/water ratio)*
*2 dashes Peychaud's bitters*
*2-3 dashes absinthe or anise-flavored spirit*
*Twist of lemon*

*In a glass or Boston shaker, combine rye, sugar syrup, and bitters over ice and stir for roughly 30 seconds. In a pre-chilled rocks glass, pour anise spirit and swirl to coat interior, pouring out any excess. Strain the cocktail into glass, squeeze lemon twist over drink, rub peel side onto the rim, then discard the twist or plop it into the glass.*

The first wheels through me like a jilted woman in a short red dress cleaving at a bonfire with a 7-iron. The second pumps the floodwater from my gem mine of a laugh, smashes out the teeth of my efficiency, hydrants on toward the capitol. I can feel the governor's ermine pelt perplex, can see the state senators splayed on the floor of the rotunda, ducking and doused and dumbshat. A third and I need to put *Dolittle* on. I need to turn it up. A third and *Debaser* dances the outrage up through the phantom roots of my babyteeth and snaggleteeth and eggteeth and dogteeth, my tongue flop-sweats, my palate uncleansed, molars grinding each other down to toothdust and rootpulp, canines towering over my anxious erosion like Tetons. A fourth and *Tame* drives the futon from the wall, clears the domestic flail of desperate breakables. I whale on the wall, whale on the wall, whale on the wall for a minute fifty-five. I take a screwdriver to the shit refrigerator. I take a screwdriver to its fat, gassy coils and let the refrigerant bleed from its cold mouth to mine. A fifth and *you think I'm dead but I've sailed away on a wave of mutilation, a wave of mutilation, a wave of mutilation, a wave, wave.*

## Dear
## Corporation,

The sirens of the city are only unmuzzled in emergencies, so they've never had a chance to tell you how much they envy the way you cry so quietly to yourself, how strong you are for having vowed to never let anyone glimpse that snap and slip of loneliness you consider a glitch in your system, how they envy the way you always find a quiet corner of the party to drink your shyness into sadness, then sit alone near the lake until dawn, trying to parse how anyone can not feel sad at a party where everyone was told to wear a bowtie and is.

## Dear
## Corporation,

Say the senator meets you in the lobby of your building. Say he stretches out his hand. Say there is something midwestern vampiric about him: a glow of suspirian blood in his sockets, an oil spill of Nick Cave hair. Say he holds your hand more firmly than he should, never breaking eye contact. Say he thanks you and thanks you and you don't know why, takes you by the elbow, and guides you to the elevator. Say when the doors close his body unspines and slips unclouded and molten into the cavities of its self, into the cavities of your self. Say you come to on the balcony at a table cluttered with the bare, shucked shells of cherrystones, littlenecks, wellfleets, a hunk of that sturgeon with the crème fraîche and bacon-infused breadcrumbs you love so much. Say the senator is gone but has conjured a 200-year-old bottle of pinot noir scavenged from a shipwreck in the Baltic Sea. Say it uncorks itself and reaches out to you with the mouthfeel of a makeshift hospital, an undimmable bouquet of evac and silencer and signal flare. Say there are catshit notes, throatcut notes, notes of shrapnel and cinder. Say the balcony beckons and you swoon to the railing and 32 stories below the floodlights erupt. Thousands of people chanting at the chainlink. Say they all go mute at once. Say they all look up at you, searching for the shade of a new false father, the dawn of a brighter deceiver.

## *Dear Corporation,*

Bullets breathe through the sky of my mouth and my teeth record it all: caplets of momentary light strafing twilit buildings. Or is it a blur of countryside? A bright district of popular cafes? The body of a whale dis-incorporating at the bottom of the sea? This is the American trick we play on top of the very own trick of our blood: we place our cameras just far enough away to convince ourselves the people we are uncoiling are not really people at all. We dismiss the death as tape glitch and lens flare and faulty intelligence, as garbled facts on the ground. We dismiss the damage as a deep dissolve and dust motes dancing in the smooth of the steadicam. I could tell you this is the safety we should all be afraid of. I could tell you we should all have the guts to look each person in the eye before we rechristen them collateral. But who am I to judge when I don't have the guts to face this world on its own crude terms. Who am I to argue against the self-defense of keeping distance, of keeping discrete. Who am I to decide whether it's healthy for drone pilots to be able to drive home each night and have dinner with their families or if some moral bond with their target is lost forever through such disconnection. And who am I to decide that one of those possibilities necessarily excludes the other. The body of a whale disincorporating at the bottom of the sea is a city of thousands of creatures alive solely because of its disincorporation. I'm the one who can tell you to your face that I believe in moral absolutes but, if pressed, not exactly what those absolutes are. I'm the one who wakes up each morning awash in avenues of avoidance. I'm the one who erases, deletes, minimizes, revises, and swipes away, who changes the channel, hits mute, closes his eyes, plugs his ears, leaves the room, heaves the flatscreen through the window, takes an axe to the laptop, the cable box, the medieval basement of breakers, who rips all the cables and cords and surge protectors from the walls and cauterizes their necks so their heads can never grow back. I'm the one that

MESSAGE MAY BE WRITTEN ON THIS SIDE

# POST CARD

ADDRESS ONLY ON THIS SIDE

Dear Corporation,

Each proud morning ███████
flashes its bleached
asshole at us, and bless
thine ass, darling, you
call it a dawning.

xo
-A.

WEST VIRGINIA
1863
FOREVER USA

## *Dear Corporation,*

Walked to The Gold Cane on Haight Street with Russell for a High Life and Powers. The Preakness began and ended while I was in the bathroom. There is a flock of end-of-the-world bar crawlers here, but I can't tell how ironic the participants are, can't tell whether they are joyously dismissing the prospect of the Rapture or joyously embracing it. The billboards and the curse-peeled, corpse-gray AM radio preachers here are predicting the end times tomorrow. They say they've calculated the numbers, called in their experts, done the due diligence, and now they clatter and coif in the static, they call the fire down mercifully to smite us. These people are more than happy to be done with people like us, happy that they will finally get what they deserve, that *we* will finally get what *we* deserve, and that their idea of who deserves what will turn out to be the same as God's.

And it's not that I order another beer and write you this letter because I believe them, or I don't believe them, or that I don't, in moments of weakness, believe there is the possibility the preachers might be right this time, it's not because I am unfaithful or unforgiven or because I am repulsed by the idea of smiling down gleefully at our own destruction, but because I refuse to let myself be separated from all of you who have so miraculously let yourselves be swept up for a moment at a time by my happy sea of blood.

## *Dear Corporation,*

Since I am drunk and
unable to use the word *smite* in any kind
of clever way, I can tell you more directly:
I normally take my bourbon neat, like
you, but this dirty city summer scalds
every throat in its limited custody and
ice and soda get me less drunk, which is,
I realize, an epic sweep of self-deception,
but our tummies are so dystopian, our
futures so distended, don't we deserve to
end up in the gift shop of self-deceit at
least one night a week? Don't we deserve
to deify Forgetting for a minute or so at
a time?

I guess what I mean is
that I was feeling self-conscious about
my last letter to you, about adulterating
my bourbon in your eyes, with your
eyes. I'm not sure why, so let me get my
wolf cub teeth right into the deer heart

of our matter: there is a brimming and braveness and feral intelligence to you that I'm taken with. Where I suspect a wilderness may be, a wilderness usually is, and I can't help but explore. My dear Corporation, you are the PJ Harvey of the investment-banking world, the Margaret Atwood of subprime mortgage lenders. You say you are unfamiliar with the taste of man, but I know a dive bar in Red Hook that proves you a liar.

## Dear
## Corporation,

I know nothing
about relief, but I do know that
relieving oneself in the limp, February
landscaping of a semi-famous poet,
passing out amongst the dead perennials
and peat and smut-smelling deerfood, is
nothing to be ashamed of. The way your
mind is disordered is the way my mind
is disordered. I love that about us! Look:
no one deserves anxiety like a flock of
geese in the turbine of a 747. No one
deserves a nervous system strung up
from the neighborhood gutters, from
the neighborhood trees, like demonic
christmas lights, but if one of us burns
out, the whole wracked string of us goes.
You ruined your night. Fine. It was just
a night. You had *just a night*. I'm sorry
for that, I am, but it's time to get you
up and get you home, time to unburr
the motion lights from your shadow

and stand you up above your own body's pause in the snow-muted mulch. Time to remind yourself of all the good people calling, falling, freaking, bailing, dishing, putting, wiping, zoning, stumbling, selling, cashing, lashing, passing out alone somewhere tonight in the jury-rigged dark. All of them and all of us just wanting someone to love us enough to pass out in the wrecklings of our flowerbeds. There are only two reasons to stop drinking. This is neither.

## Dear Corporation,

The headlights that come for me tonight are photocopies of photographs of headlights in storms so dark I hid in the basement with my brother. I drive home through a subdivision that was a cornfield last year, find private jets perched in the trees, their tail lights softening the streets, wingspans tenderizing houses like meat. They snip at the roof tiles with de-iced beaks, civilians grasped in their landing gear, pressurized in their bellies, CEOs asleep in their seats or checking their stocks on laptops. The night air is thick with the trills of intercom chatter, the hum of blackbox recorders. I want to give in, pull over, make an offering of all my electronics, my belt and my shoes, my arms spread wide for the wand. I want to be digested by the dim of their cabin lights. But I keep driving. Somewhere

up ahead, I know there is a catalpa
waiting for me, a text message from you
gouged in its bark, a heart carved around
it, pierced by an arrow.

## Dear Corporation,

I was about to smash my hand through the shatterproof glass of another disheveled college town Halloween, but this girl walked past in a self-made mustard bottle costume, scissor-shredded stockings, wobbling in stilettos like a newborn giraffe. I'm not sure if it's that I couldn't tell where the eyeholes were, or couldn't tell how she was steering, or my logistical confusion about how she could possibly deal with the bulk of the weight all night, how she'd sip from her flask or bong a beer or use the restroom, that melted the irrational judgment from me, but thank god she walked by because I needed so desperately to be melted.

I'm scared sometimes that my default setting is *Asshole* and in my inability to escape it, I fling my tedious, uninteresting judgments upon others as a way of deflecting my own culpability. So I want to take this opportunity to apologize to all of you right now and if you are out on the streets this weekend pretending to be something other than yourself or strategically revealing your true self for the first time, please be safe. Try to stick to one kind of alcohol. Smile politely at the police officers and their huge, skittery horses. Remind yourself that we're all wearing blinders and being driven by forces outside of our control. Avoid rolling blackouts of aggressive drunks, roving fogs of pepper spray, and raving bands of terrible music. Avoid shattered glass and men dressed as The Joker from *The Dark Knight* (though hug anyone dressed as Jack Nicholson's 1989 version of the same). If you need me, I'll be at home listening to *Silence Yourself, Transcendental Youth, Strange Mercy,* mixing makeshift Manhattans, and working on *Adam Fell's Untitled Young Adult Zombie Apocalypse Novel.* Don't hesitate to call if you need a ride home or a hand up or a health pack, if you need a band-aid or sutures or a swab of disinfectant, a stiff drink or an airbed or a dryer-fresh blanket. Don't let the bastards grind you down. You are a grace-filled, splitfoot demon clopping sparks up from this backward, blackout city.

# *Dear Corporation,*

The morning after the Tohoku tsunami destroyed the eastern coast of Japan, killing more than 16,000 people and causing the Fukushima Daiichi nuclear power plant to melt down, I woke up hung over in Wisconsin, my body leaking like a lacerated radiator. And as I toddled to the bathroom, a retired Buddhist undertaker was carefully gathering the first of a thousand bodies from what the ocean had left behind, clearing the mud from each mouth and throat, massaging each stiff limb living soft for identification.

Where the sky had always been they had last seen ocean, and I don't know why I feel the need to apologize. Is this a guilt I feel? A shame at not having suffered? A lack of purpose? Are there human things I'm not involved in that I am complicit in? For three years, I was in love with distracting myself from being a part of even the most ephemeral communities. Like those stalker flowers always tracking the pulpy arc of the sun, my brain only bent toward the pillow, the stereo, the book, or the bottle. I held grudges, made judgments, imploded into the cellular signal of collateral light, and collapsed in on myself like some vast internal sun. I forgot who I had always tried to be and came to drinking rye in my underwear on a February porch, convinced that each flake of falling snow was a shred of the only document that could help me make sense of whatever that whistleblower of a winter was trying to tell me, if only I could gather the pieces into just the right order, if only they wouldn't melt at my touch.

I am far away now. I don't see the same fraying strands of

people anymore. I remember most of my life in memories the fidelity of crinkled VCR tape. I have unspooled myself on the sidewalk and my immediate, American days have only a grainy, garbled newsfeed's conception of the overwhelming sense of helplessness and serenity, insignificance and irrepressible power, a person must feel finding the ocean where there had ever only been sky. Maybe I shouldn't even be trying to imagine what it was like, but this is what happens to us, against our own best judgment, though also perhaps for the best. We watch video clips of the ocean sweeping in, the cruise ships and yachts and cars swept away like stray recycling. The people are there too, thousands of them, just too small to see on the screen, and I imagine not what each of them must be feeling but how I would have felt in their place and I can't tell anymore if that is the height of empathy or selfishness. There is so much unexpected ego even in this line of self-interrogation that, reading back, I'm astonished and ashamed. And no matter what I think or feel or what beliefs I eventually click on or away from, here is the truth: I'll wake up tomorrow in a progressive, college town in the upper midwest of America and walk out in the spring sun to post this letter to you, the one person I know I can say anything to, the one person I know will not judge me for the failure of these words to convey what I truly mean, who will not judge me for not knowing what I believe anymore, who knows how easily words can become the most inscrutable pathogens in their passing, and there will be sky above me, and living people I love, dark wingbeats of anxious air atoning our lungs.

Dear Corporation,

I hope we'll see
each other again on the far
side of security; slip each
other's belts back through their
loops, tie each other's shoes,
tuck each other's more
charming ablutions carefully back
into the pockets of our own
baggage.

Love, A. ➡

## Dear
## Corporation,

I know I will never
outlive this gritting on the pale
plasticulate of my own culpability.
I know I will never outlast this too-
human season of proms. There is too
much money involved, too much power
at stake, and I can't stop watching,
waiting indignantly for our glitch and
kick to crash the connection, to redact
the comments about comments about
comments. So I walk to the record
store, stumble through the used bins.
*Purple Rain, Reckoning, Staring at
the Sea.* On the way home I skirt the
capitol building, trying to discern which
window the governor is shattering out at
us from behind. The LPs unwrapped are
lightless nights of water. They have their
own tidal pull in my hands. Untapped
like this, their currents are glyphs that
glance the buildings back as curves of

fractured light. I hold the city by its edges, find the smudges of other people's fingers, the nicks and skips and scratches of staunchly spinning years. Thank god there's at least one thing we can all agree on: scars are left by even the most delicate love.

## Dear
## Corporation,

On the balcony of the
32nd floor, you stand hand in hand
with your brother for the first time in
months. Asshole college girl's arrow
still slotting his throat, Colorado soccer
scarf carving its dark red rapids through
the kindness of his shoulders, his eyes
like spilt bottled water. You love him to
death, though you do not talk, you text.
The moon wavers like a tattered flag on
the surface of the infinity pool.

You don't open the
bottle, the bottle opens you, and you
both drink in Forgetting for a moment,
and, for a moment, you almost forgive
yourselves. Your hand on your brother's
shoulder and he passes the bottle. Never
wipe the lip. Drink deep. Once. Twice.
Stand together at the railing. Look out
through the smoke, over the distance of

fires, the protesters surging like night-drawn bison through the free speech zone. Drink to the longest health and love of each other. Drink to your parents in their terraced garden of retirement. Drink to your friends and their signal flare eyes and the crass electricities that keep you in touch. Drink to the sirens slinking from somewhere below you to somewhere below you, the wind rushing up to the penthouse bringing all the human smells no mint can mask.

## Dear
## Corporation,

On any normal night the fourth drink is a plutocratic dystopia: you either become the robber baron or the rabble. But tonight the crawling fog of bourbon and exhaustion tune you to some strange and spectral station. Behind the static, there are the sounds of a senator alone with a shotgun in his study. Slippers hushed on a bearskin rug, the crackling of book after book in the fireplace. There is the kiss and flare and strike of unexpected lightning, then the chattering of a cocktail party at the bottom of a pool. Your brother's voice falls down to you from Denver, warm with dark rum and Winterfell. *Chopped and screwed*, his tape-glitch voice skips down through the ceiling fan, *chopped and screwed*, and then, above it all, Sarah singing Loretta Lynn in the bedroom as she waits for her bacon and eggs.

You can't help but feel in their cascade of voices how heavy the world is, how galloping and gorgeous and unshoulderable, a world that revels in the breadth and breathlessness of its own disincorporation. It's a world that knows you never said goodbye to your grandfather, sure, but knows you never really said hello either, knows you never asked him about his first date with Grandma, never asked him about the Freemasons because you didn't know he was a Freemason until the strange, white-gloved host of men sitting sepulchrally behind you at the funeral began to sing and fill his casket with evergreen fronds. And now, above the voices you love and the subtle cutlery of dead air between stations, you swear you can hear him whisper-whistling the same irretrievable ghost song he always did, a song you never asked the name of, that grows clearer and clearer until it's as if you are both the same age in the same classroom, as if after 32 years, the signal of your cells has finally synched up with the people you come from. The bullet smelter and brass polisher and lunch lady. The vegetable farmer and inn keeper and machinist. The small town cinema projectionist and your parents, the school psychologists. And you realize that this is not some familial epiphany, nor some siren song or clarion call to find out where you come from, because their lives, no matter who your people were or what they did or what you should have asked them, are buried like a bright, unbreakable knife, blade up in your middle-western blood.

## Dear Corporation,

The man has his gray hoodie up, his back to me through the bar's convalescing window. It's July but the man shocks ragged on the corner like a mammoth thawed living from ice. He stumbles in front of an old storefront that is no longer a storefront but a respite for recuperating adults. A place to eat and to sleep, to converse and conserve. A place to weather hell and help others and heal.

Or so I have been told. All I truly know is that the man in gray bends down to the sidewalk and picks up something too small for me to see. A pebble or a shard of glass. A lost eyelash or lost tooth or lost marble or the plucked-out eye of a pink, half-burnt teddy bear. Whatever it is, whether a useless thing or an urgent thing, a figment or fixed or fluid shape, the man casts the maybe object up toward a shade-drawn, second story window. He waits impatiently for his expected response. When it doesn't come, he bounces on his boot heels, waves a gruff, dismissive hand at the window, pelts the air with an epidemic of backhands.

He bends down, picks up nothing-or-something and casts it again. This time, the light is different, or the wind, and the nothing-or-something darkens then glints into full, true thingness half way through its arc, bouncing from the pane of the still-drawn window, vanishing again on the fall. The man waits. Again, no answer. He spreads his arms wide to the window as if he can't contemplate a world where this unresponsiveness is fact. Or can't contemplate a response that is not his preferred response. Or that the meeting of his expectation could possibly depend

on the pure jugular pull of another's
tide of blood; a heart behind a shade
two stories up that he believes he knows
but does not. He reaches up toward the
window, palms meeting in prayer or in
protest, then reaches down to pick up
the small object again.

My dear Corporation,
happy hour is almost over. On the table,
my bourbon sogs through its coaster.
Ice cubes melt in the air conditioning.
I don't know if you've been listening. I
don't know if these letters are getting
through or being redacted or shredded
or tossed unopened into the fire, but this
stumbling man and his crushing need to
be heard, to be understood and answered
as an equal, is all I have left and I will
hurl it at your window forever through
the shredded raw of my throat.

XO always,
    -A.

# INDEX OF FIRST LINES

# ACKNOWLEDGEMENTS

This book is dedicated to Sarah Kinser, who loves the world and hates the world as much as I do. Thank god.

To Sue, Larry, and Tyler Fell; Grandma and Grandpa Fell; Grandma Schmidt; and all my family, ancestors, and antecedents: thank you for all of your love and hard work and the middle-western blood in my veins. My love always.

A huge and ardent thank you to the following publications for previously unleashing selections from this book into the world, sometimes in quite different versions: Bridge Poetry Series; *Diagram*; the Dorothy Sargent Rosenberg Prize; *Forklift, Ohio*; *H_NGM_N*; *Hell Yes Press* and their rad 21 *Love Poems* mixtape project; *Ink Node*; *iO Poetry*; *jubilat*; *The Lumberyard*; *Matter*; *Ocean State Review*; *Phantom Limb*; *Pinwheel*; *Poetry City, USA, Vol.* 3; and Poets.org.

This book would not have been possible without:

Nate & Thea Brown; Katie Byrum; Eric Caldera; Kara Candito; Victor Castro; Jordan Cohen; Mary Anne & Mike Cowgill; Nick Demske; Russell Dillon; Keara Driscoll; Dobby Gibson; The Gildings; Kevin González; Gracie; Matthew Guenette; Matt Hart; Brenda Hillman; Daniel Khalastchi; Ben Kopel; Jane Lewty; Macha the Chuch; Madé, King of Dogs; Erika Meitner; Christopher Mohar; Becca Myers; Caryl Pagel; Sarah Polenska; Srikanth Reddy; Dan Rosenberg; Lauren Shapiro; Michael Sheehan; Ellen Siebers; Nate Slawson; Amanda Smeltz; Sara Jane Stoner; Barrett Edward Swanson; Ryan Walsh; Dean Young.

Edgewood College—especially the wonderful English faculty and students; The Council for Wisconsin Writers and Shake Rag Alley; and Stephen Lovely and the astounding students, faculty, and counselors at the Iowa Young Writers' Studio.

M.T. Anderson; Apollinaire; Margaret Atwood; William Basinski; David Berman; The Binding of Isaac; Roberto Bolaño; Breaking Bad; Califone; Italo Calvino; Chromatics; Louis CK; the Crystal Corner Bar; Dark Souls; Deadwood; Drive; Russ Feingold; Fez; Frightened Rabbit; Lauren

Groff; GZA/Genius; Journey (the video game); Joy Division; Kentucky Route Zero; Etheridge Knight; Limbo; Loretta Lynn; Maduro; Cormac McCarthy; David Milch; Chelsey Minnis; David Mitchell; Mountain Goats; My Bloody Valentine; The National; Neutral Milk Hotel; Nirvana; Frank Ocean; Osteria Papavero and their transcendent lunch specials; Pixies; Christopher Priest; Radiohead; Marjane Satrapi; George Saunders; Savages; St. Vincent; Justice John Paul Stevens; Andrei Tarkovsky; Titus Andronicus; The Walkmen; The Weary Traveler; Winter's Bone; and James Wright.

# NOTES

The epigraph "Nolite te bastardes carborundorum" is from Margaret Atwood's novel *The Handmaid's Tale*. It is a mock-Latin phrase that is carved by the previous handmaid into the floor of Offred's closet. It translates to "Don't let the bastards grind you down."

*"Tyger, listen, we're burning too bright already..."* is forever in debt to the love and art and blood and beat of The Pagel Family, Russell Dillon, Nick Demske, William Blake, Italo Calvino, The Clash, Prince, Resident Evil 2, Alex Proyas, Loretta Lynn, Fallout 3, Erik Larson, David Bowie, PJ Harvey, Chromatics, China Miéville, Wolf Parade, The Legend of Zelda: Ocarina of Time, The Hold Steady, Erika Meitner, Bruce Springsteen, The Walkmen, The Clash (again), Lucinda Williams, Gram Parsons, Half-Life 2, James Tate, Jean-Pierre Jeunet and Marc Caro, Fernando Meirelles, Broadcast, Talking Heads, Modest Mouse, and Savages. Rick Santorum, however, can go fuck himself.

*"No one likes their first cigarette."* contains lyrics from "In the Air Tonight" by Phil Collins.

*"When I go for a run, the strangest violence glows..."* contains lyrics from "Wave of Mutilation" by Pixies, and references song titles from their album, *Dolittle*. The Sazerac recipe in the poem is an adapation of a recipe from *Garden and Gun* magazine, February/March 2012.

The photograph on Postcard #3 (part of which was adapted for the front cover design) used with the kind permission of Nancy Sanders and Sarah Kinser.

The author photo is courtesy of Amanda Manteufel.

Adam Fell is the author of *I Am Not a Pioneer* (Hangman Books), winner of the 2011 Posner Best Poetry Book Award from the Council for Wisconsin Writers.

He lives in Madison, Wisconsin where he teaches at Edgewood College and co-curates the Monsters of Poetry Reading Series.

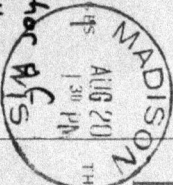

MADISON
AUG 20
1 30 PM
WIS

www.ingramcontent.com/pod-product-compliance
Lightning Source LLC
LaVergne TN
LVHW091226080426
835509LV00009B/1188